WEST BROMWICH
IN OLD PHOTOGRAPHS

THE SWAN VILLAGE OFF-LICENCE OF ALFRED KIRKHAM operated from the early 1920s until it closed in 1956. Mrs Laura Kirkham (right) stands outside No. 34b William Street which also sold tobacco and groceries.

WEST BROMWICH
IN OLD PHOTOGRAPHS

COMPILED BY
ROBIN PEARSON

ALAN SUTTON
1989

Alan Sutton Publishing
Gloucester

First published 1989

British Library Cataloguing in Publication Data

West Bromwich in old photographs.
1. West Midlands (Metropolitan County). West Bromwich, history
I. Pearson, Robin
942.4'94

ISBN 0-86299-672-4

Typesetting and origination by
Alan Sutton Publishing
Printed in Great Britain by
Dotesios Printers Limited.

CONTENTS

To the memory of
Douglas Dilworth
George Jones
and
Richard Ludgate
who all did much
to record the history of
West Bromwich

INTRODUCTION

A populous and widely spread village in a parish of the same name, in the hundred of Offlow South, is about 116 miles from London, and 2 south east of Wednesday; situated in a county abounding with inexhaustible mines of iron and coal, that run in all directions beneath the parish, and afford by their produce and workings materials for flourishing manufactures, and employment to a great population. Only a few years ago, that portion of the parish where is situated the principal part of the village, was but a heath, in which rabbits burrowed in great numbers: such a place is not now to be recognized; the habitations of men, and establishments of artisans, have sprung up with surprising rapidity; and, from a place insignificant in its origin, West Bromwich has become important in its trade and manufactures, with a population enterprising and respectable.

Thus *Pigot's Directory of Staffordshire* for 1828/9 described the future town that would be incorporated in 1882. In the period up to this event the population would rise from about 14,000 to over 56,000. Such a steady growth in the citizenry was attributable to an equally dramatic increase in the range of trade and industries throughout the area.

A hundred years ago the town was producing 'axle boxes and hollow shafts, fenders, fireirons, locks, bolts, hinges, nails, saddlers' ironmongery, coach furniture, spring balances and steam gauges, iron culinary utensils, chains, traces, spades, steel toys, saucepan handles, railway pins, hollow ware, scale beams, patten rings, coffee mills, horse shoes, roasting jacks, gas holders, gas tubes and fittings, water pipes, palisades, and ornamental iron work of every kind'. Industrial premises included not only 'furnaces for smelting of iron ore, foundries, forges, and slitting mills but also maltings, brass foundries, boat yards, lime kilns, a tar distillery, washing and baking powder manufactories, brick yards etc.'

West Bromwich came of age at a time of Victorian industrial and commercial pride. The leaders of local industry felt it their duty to contribute by actively giving of their time for participation in municipal affairs. The Chamberlains and Cadburys in neighbouring 'Bromycham' (Birmingham) gave the lead in assuming civic responsibilities. West Bromwich leaders of industry wanted to 'make the lives of the people brighter and happier'.

Reuben Farley was the archetypal municipal do-gooder whose generosity to his native town knew no bounds. He gave land for a public park in Whitehall Road near to his birthplace because he had such 'an abiding affection for the place of his birth and one expression of it was his gift of Farley Park'. He also persuaded the Dartmouths to provide land for what was to become Dartmouth Park.

But what of the lot of the people? The iron trade offered hard work to those who could stand the heat and exertion. Wages were often paid out at the local pub where there was much opportunity for eating and drinking. Some foundries operated an even more notorious system of a 'tommy' shop whereby workers were paid in tokens or vouchers only exchangeable for goods from those establishments in which the employers naturally had a stake. Happily, such practices were eventually outlawed.

With wages paid out on Saturdays, the nineteenth-century High Street must have been quite a sight. All the shops stayed open late that night and were brilliantly lit to attract customers. People in the lowest income bracket waited for last minute bargains – an opportunity to acquire the Sunday joint in some sort of Dutch auction as butchers sought to sell off their remaining meat. 'Come on, missus, what shall I say for this? A bob, elevenpence, tenpence, ninepence – here, take it for a tanner!'

Dusty 'smoke-dried habitations' were the lot of people forced to live in the back to back houses found on The Lyng. Various roads such as Dove Street, formerly called Duffill, are shown in this book as a reminder of those times when water was drawn by a pump from a well in the backyard.

Victorian novelist, David Christie Murray, described Lyng residents in his many books that drew on experiences of his native West Bromwich. Workers relaxed over a pint 'clad in thick flannel jackets, thrown open to show the gaudy lining of cheap felt carpeting, heavy ankle jack-boots, mostly worn unlaced with a big crumpled tongue hanging out, as though the boots were thirstier than their wearers, nondescript hats of felt, shaped like basins and without a pretence of brim'. Murray also noted that the dangers of working life were taken for granted by these artisans. 'It was noticeable that most of these men were blazoned in a single manner on the face as if they had been tattooed and the design had been half obliterated. Each man so marked had felt Death's hand upon his cheek once at least.'

Another novelist described in harsh terms the seemingly awful 'grimy desolation' of streets where the metals trade had its heart. Grice Street was described as 'Rusty Lane' by J.B. Priestley in his famous book, *English Journey*; an account of his travels throughout the length of the country in the 1930s.

Perhaps the famous writer was a little harsh on West Bromwich for it was work in these severe conditions that gave the Black Country a sense of prosperity. Many firms did attempt to improve the working environment of their employees. Such philanthropy was not only from a Victorian sense of religous duty but also a realization that a contented workforce produced a better product!

The ironfounders, Bagnalls, were such an example of the paternal approach. They provided housing and even a church complete with a clergyman – an early example of an industrial chaplaincy. The children of their workers attended a school built by the company. This educational establishment was run on such efficient lines that it attracted the attention of a government commission on education which praised such provision.

Another company which, unlike the Bagnal firm, survives today after a benevolent approach towards its employees is Salter's. The works football team called *The Strollers* later developed into the internationally known stars – West Bromwich Albion.

While the spring trade survives and flourishes, other industries have died through the exhaustion of natural resources or competition from more advanced and changed methods of manufacture. Iron ore and coal were exploited early in West Bromwich's industrial development. A pit such as Hamstead continued extracting coal until March 1965. There is still an estimated 20 million ton potential remaining underground but geological faults make it impossible to mine anymore.

West Bromwich, despite its original extensive area, always had wider territorial ambitions. Wednesbury always appeared as the potential target of such schemes, as in 1908 and 1921. Even before and after the Second World War Wednesbury still felt threatened. In 1966 West Bromwich was finally triumphant when the Black Country local government reorganization saw a union with Tipton and Wednesbury.

For West Bromwich its period as a larger authority was short-lived. In 1974 Sandwell was created after the government's nationwide restructuring of local administrations. While other towns and villages were absorbed into their bigger neighbours of Dudley, Walsall and Wolverhampton, the amalgamation of Warley (itself seen by some as a false union of three historic towns) with West Bromwich presented a problem over the choice of name for the new metropolitan borough. Sandwell may be a historic apellation but to many people it has a 'fiction-like' quality. The recent proposal for city status has provoked a lively debate with many wanting a revival of the real name that has 'identity, history and notability' – West Bromwich.

BARRAGE BALLOON tethered over Sandwell Road at its junction with Beale Street 1939.

SECTION ONE

'The Golden Mile'

'This street – which has the advantage of being the great thoroughfare from Birmingham to Wolverhampton – is without doubt the Sackville Street of the Black Country. It is broad, straight, well-paved, and flanked on either side with buildings which are imposing in a two-fold sense, for many of them appear to be stone, while in reality they are stucco. It sustains a brisk traffic all day long. Parasols make a fair display this summer-time, and vehicles of every grade, from the potato cart and upwards, are whirling to and fro on business or pleasure. Indeed, the whole aspect of the street is just the antipodes of an ordinary Black Country thoroughfare, and by a little stretch of imagination one might suppose that the white-painted buildings on either hand belonged to some smart country town'. Thus the Birmingham Daily Gazette *of 1 June 1868 waxed lyrical about England's longest High Street. The comparison with the British Isles' widest street of Georgian elegance was perhaps a large 'stretch of imagination'.*

The early photographs certainly capture something of that sense of bustle but, as motor traffic increased, the Street seemed to be returning to what novelist David Christie Murray described as 'rather doleful'. His perception of a straggling thoroughfare has reappeared with the pedestrianization of the middle section.

A local MP has pressed for the Birmingham end to be given a facelift that would match the recent revamping of the pedestrian section which has created one of the Black Country's most popular shopping centres.

TURN OF THE CENTURY VIEW of what is now the top end of the pedestrian zone, with the Farley Fountain from Dartmouth Park relocated close to its original site.

AT SAMUEL COOKSON'S SHOP the ladies' version of 'it' cost five shillings extra.

THE VIEW FROM SCOTLAND PASSAGE looking north in 1956.

SANDWELL HOUSE on the corner of Trinity Road was a hotel and later a boys' school. The present day 'Sandwell' was at that time called the 'Birmingham House'.

THIS GARAGE, still in use today through the archway, adjoined the 'Lewisham Hotel'.

HARRY KENDALL moved from Spon Lane to this shop, the first of his High Street premises.

ELECTRIC PALACE CINEMA (left at No. 204), 1972, prior to demolition. Films were shown from 1910 until 1957. The entrance was next to Burtons Tailoring – originally the way in from Paradise Street.

EDWARD HEELIS, originally a Manxman, found his time as mayor such a financial burden that he was forced to sell his business to George Mason's.

A VIEW from Hudson's Passage 1965.

TWO VIEWS, 60 years apart, looking towards the Town Hall.

THE MARKET HALL, built in 1874, proved to be a commercial failure as people preferred the traditional open air markets higher up the town. It was demolished and the site used for a new library (below).

THE OFFICIAL OPENING, in 1907, of the 'monumental but not large' building – the gift to the town from Andrew Carnegie, the universal benefactor of libraries.

GEORGE WAKELAM, a member of a family of local boot makers, operated his business for over 30 years from No. 57 High Street.

QUEEN STREET corner with the appropriately named public house in 1965. Below, a view in 1974 looking further up the High Street prior to pedestrianization.

EARLY SIXTIES TRAFFIC north and south of St Michael Street.

THE KENRICK & JEFFERSON building provides a background to public transport 50 years apart.

DARTMOUTH GARAGE, established in 1904, undergoing alterations in 1959. The company was taken over in 1976 by Charles Clarke.

THE DAYS OF TRANSISTOR MANIA in this 1965 view.

ORIGINALLY BUILT AS COTTAGES in the early 1800s, these shops have been replaced between Bull Street and Water Street.

THIS MODEL T FORD was bought in 1925 by John Cunningham to replace his pony and trap.

THE OLD POST OFFICE, near Dartmouth Street, opened in 1828 with Thomas Sutton as postmaster. Ten years earlier Hannah Sutton ran the post office at Hill Top. Samuel Sutton ran the service from 1841 until the closure of this building as an office in 1868.

'LYE' TYPE TRAM waits on Dartmouth Square, November 1929.

ALSO NEAR DARTMOUTH SQUARE the triumphant Albion team home with the 1931 FA Cup.

ALBION WON THE FA CUP FINAL in May 1954 and the team was treated to a civic reception.

JOHN ALLEN dealt in pianos at No. 284 and then No. 233 for a quarter of a century.

NO. 247 HIGH STREET around 1900.

SECTION TWO

At Work

Working days at the turn of the century were long, starting at 6 a.m. and finishing at 5 p.m. with perhaps 1½ hours off for breaks during that time. The metal trades were the founding basis of West Bromwich's economic growth. After the decline of the South Staffordshire iron trade as natural resources ran out, it was ironfounding and later steel making that soon expanded the local industrial base.

Canals in the eighteenth century allowed the collieries to sell their coal. When the canal through Golds Hill and Golds Green opened in 1796 the price of coal in Birmingham dropped from 13s. to 7s. 6d. a ton. Later the railway allowed a more rapid importing of raw materials and the export of finished products. Sidings and rail lines into factory sites were commonplace. The Albion Iron Works was served by both canal and railway.

Not only were the hours long but much of the local work was dangerous. Accidents were frequent, none more so than in the mines that once provided much local employment. The Hamstead Colliery disaster of 1908 was one such tragedy in which 25 men lost their lives.

Just as nailing has passed into the working memory so has another industry disappeared. Millions of blue paving bricks were supplied to Birmingham Corporation and smaller quantities went into the construction of London's Tower Bridge.

ALBION IRON WORKS were erected around 1840 by Walter Williams 'at a great cost and in the most substantial manner'.

THE RAIL MILL at Albion Works in August 1859 while, below, sections for the Parahybema Bridge are prepared.

37

IZONS, one of the area's oldest firms, came to dominate the hollow-ware business. The easy availability of local water power to drive machinery allowed the installation of a Boulton and Watt beam engine, only the second such made by the famous company.

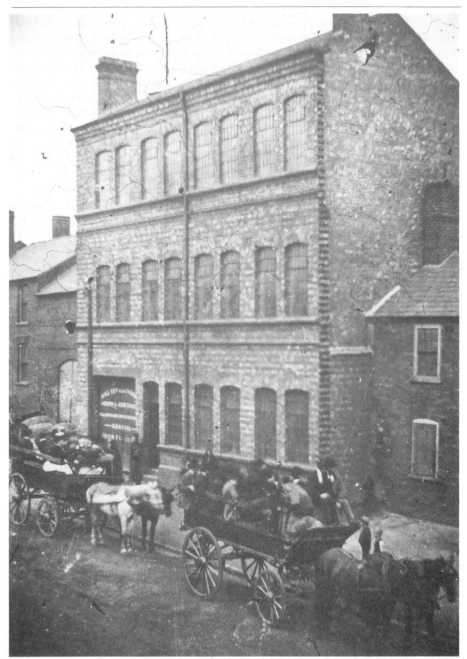

COUSINS JOSEPH AND JESSE SIDDONS established their Hill Top Foundry in 1848 at this three-storey building, seen here in around 1870, opposite the Sow and Pigs Inn. In 1878 the company started operations on a bigger site.

J. & S. ROBERTS operated at Swan Village until 1904 producing mostly grain and chilled rolls seen in the photographs. The man with the umbrella (left above), also seen top right below, was the colourful local character, John Clayton, builder of nearby 'Clayton's Folly'.

SUNDAY BEST for the above employees of Henry Boot & Sons during work on the Tantany Estate in 1921/2.

JOSEPH GUEST & SONS of Henry Street — employees in summer 1933.

SLUDGE DISPOSAL onto derelict land while Swan Farm marlhole (below) was used as a private tip in 1958.

BRICKMAKING was once a major industry in the Greets Green and Great Bridge (above) areas. Brickmakers (below) at Wood & Ivery Limited which produced blue bricks for use in the Elan Valley reservoirs.

HAMBLET BLUE BRICK CO. LTD. owned this deep marlhole off Wood Lane. At the height of its production in the 1890s the company was making half a million bricks a week.

JOSEPH ROTHWELL began business as a herb beer brewer at 49 Sandwell Road: horse-drawn deliveries were made in the 1920s until motor vehicles were introduced in the 1930s (below).

ROTHWELL also became a pickle manufacturer in 1921 – hence the building work. Extra premises were later acquired in Bratt Street.

FLEETS OF HORSE-DRAWN VEHICLES such as Rothwell's required harness and tackle. Although competition from the motor vehicle reduced the number of the town's saddlers this business continued up to the Second World War.

PUDDLER, Thomas Hale (left), at the Church Lane Iron Works of Johnsons Iron & Steel Co. Ltd., in around 1912.

SANDWELL PARK COLLIERY (above) was successful during the general decline in the South Staffordshire coalfield. Its success gave impetus to the development of the Hamstead Colliery (below).

JUBILEE COLLIERY — a bowk damaged during the sinking of a shaft with fatal results.

MINERS AT COLES FARM COLLIERY. Work was hard and, at most times, dangerous such as in March 1908 when 25 men were killed at the Hamstead Colliery (below).

JOHN WELSBY from Yorkshire was among the many rescuers who came to help at the Hamstead mine fire. He died attempting to reach the trapped men. His funeral was later attended by some 6,000 miners.

L OF JOHN WEL... ALTON'S HERO

WILLIAM & JOSEPH LAWLEY, ironfounders, of Sams Lane – the workforce pictured around 1910.

SECTION THREE

Party Time

Just as people worked hard, so recreation time was equally important. The so-called 'Wakes' were boisterous affairs involving much drunkenness and rowdiness. As old cruel pastimes were curtailed the provision of public facilities became important for the civic fathers. When Dartmouth Park was opened there was much celebration including fireworks and many people lined the nearby streets as dignitaries arrived. The bandstand was often surrounded by large crowds while others flocked to the boating lake. Today the parks seem almost deserted by comparison.

Vast crowds also turned out to welcome home the Albion teams who were triumphant in Cup Finals. Similarly great crowds appeared to hear proclamations read on royal occasions. Street parties were common to supplement the people's excuse for further enjoyment.

ALBION TEAM OF 1888 and trams lined up outside the Hawthorns ready for the fans in 1938.

BANDTIME in the 1920s at Kenrick & Jefferson Ltd. (above) and boys at Wigmore school.

ELECTION TIME IN 1929 (above) and 1922 (below) when F.O. Roberts the successful
candidate and his wife, right, received a rose bowl in Rydding Square.

FORMER FUN TIME revealed on old posters exposed on buildings in Spon Lane prior to demolition in 1965.

ROYAL VISIT of the Prince of Wales in June 1923
(later Edward VIII and then Duke of Windsor)
who ponders on the 'bad time in regard to
unemployment'. The Prince, accompanied by
the mayor, met a group of disabled ex-
servicemen among the crowds.

THE PRINCE with
DISABLED SOLDIERS

DARTMOUTH PARK LAKE was created on Queen Victoria's Golden Jubilee. The pavilion (above) served for many years as a refreshment room. It was destroyed by fire in April 1983.

OFFICIAL OPENINGS for the Oak House as a museum in 1898 (above) and the Sons of Rest building in Oakwood Park in 1935.

TABLEAU, FIRST PRIZE at the 1919 Horse Show.

WIGMORE SCHOOL PT team.

READING OF PROCLAMATION, by the mayor, on the accession of King George V in 1910 — everybody seems more interested in the camera.

PARADES. A suitably titled display by Kingfisher Ltd., the school furniture manufacturers, while a pennyfarthing goes by in 1935.

ROEBUCK STREET decorated for the street party (on the pavement!) to celebrate the Silver Jubilee of King George V.

LODGE ROAD – children prepare for the drive to a maypole in Dartmouth Park.

BOER WAR VETERANS MARCHING TO THE DRILL HALL for its official opening in 1903 by General John French, the future First World War army leader.

A CORPORATION BUS bedecked for the Festival of Britain.

GLOVER STREET in party mood for the Coronation of George VI.

MORE CORONATION CELEBRATIONS, June 1953: fancy dress on Tyndal Street and party in Union Street.

FILM SHOWS FOR CHILDREN at Hill Top's Rex Cinema and party time in a pub yard in Crookhay Lane, June 1953.

HOLY TRINITY JUNIOR SCHOOL is the scene for a tea party to mark Queen Elizabeth II's Silver Jubilee in 1977.

Church and Chapel

When so many Nonconformist chapels were built in the town it seemed an astonishing achievement after the difficulties encountered in the eighteenth century. The Ebenezer or Old Meeting was frequently attacked and finally burnt down by the mob. Early Methodists suffered during the riots which were at their worst in neighbouring Wednesbury. John Wesley received a friendly welcome in West Bromwich and the crowds wanting to hear him were too large for the local meeting house. He consequently preached in the open air and, on one occasion at least, in the courtyard of the Oak House.

One local resident who was attracted to Methodism was to become famous in America. Francis Asbury answered Wesley's call for someone to go and preach across the Atlantic. From 1771 until his death in 1816 he travelled thousands of miles to become the 'Prophet of the Long Road'.

Pleasant Sunday afternoons were the idea of another West Bromwich person. When young men complained about church sermons being dull John Blackham decided to do something about it. As a deacon at the Congregational Chapel he started in 1875 calling his sermons 'pleasant'. His idea was successful for over 30 years.

ALL SAINTS, known as the 'Old Church', pictured in the mid-afternoon – around 3 o'clock seemed a favourite time on many old photographs of this building. Presumably the man with the buckets was the sexton.

CHOIRS A HUNDRED YEARS APART. All Saints (above) and Wesley Chapel (below) at the 1977 'Carols by Candlelight' at the Oak House.

CHRIST CHURCH after the fire of 23 October 1979.

REVD CHARLES CARRINGTON, Vicar of Christ Church 1894–1902, pictured with his family.

ST GEORGE'S HALL, Paradise Street – a building with many uses – erected in 1806 as a Wesleyan chapel, then used as a school. In 1859 it was converted by music dealer Samuel Adams into a public hall and used as such until the advent of the Town Hall. It became a wire factory in 1891 and was turned into a cinema in 1920, showing films until 1955. It was finally demolished in 1962.

THE REVD THOMAS LORD, was Congregational minister at Salem Chapel, Great Bridge (1873–1878) when he retired at the age of 70. In 1897 he was still occasionally preaching and this 'grand old man' was featured over four columns of the front page of the local newspaper.

TWO HIGH STREET CHURCHES built and demolished within ten years of each other. The Baptist (above) one year before demolition in 1973 and the Congregational below in around 1900.

THE CATHOLIC APOSTOLIC CHURCH built this curiously shaped structure (right) in 1869–70. The building was taken over by the Elim Pentecostal Church and totally rebuilt in 1971–2. The building below had an equally curious history. It was first Methodist, then Congregational, rebuilt by the Wesleyans and acquired and reopened by the Congregationalists. Eventually it was replaced in 1932 on the opposite corner by the Allen Memorial Chapel.

THE YOUNG MEN'S CHRISTIAN ASSOCIATION operated for its first four years in West Bromwich from a coach house and stables in New Street, before moving into these premises in St Michael Street in 1888. By the time of this photograph, around 1900, it was a centre for social and educational activities. In 1970 a new hostel opened at Carter's Green.

IN THE FOLD AT OVEREND. Sister Myra Lambert preaches to Methodists, 1907.

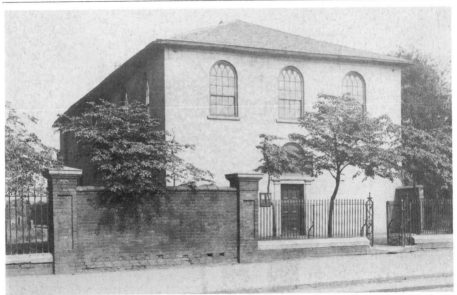

THE OLD MEETING, later Ebenezer, became a Sunday School when a new chapel was built. The former chapel pictured here was then replaced by a new building in 1906.

WESLEY CHAPEL, High Street, in 1905, later demolished and replaced by a new church in 1974.

BEECHES ROAD METHODIST CHAPEL, built in 1871/2 but no longer used as a church.

ASBURY COTTAGE, boyhood home of America's first Methodist bishop, prior to demolition of adjoining cottage for road widening.

ST PAUL'S CHURCH, Golds Hill, Sunday school anniversary parade around 1950 and, below, parish ex-servicemen assembled around 1925.

For the Public Good

The early form of local government for an area such as West Bromwich was to be found in manorial courts and then the vestry. By the mid-nineteenth century this latter body felt itself inadequate to cope with the demands made by the rapid expansion of the town. For a period of 28 years 16 improvement commissioners did much to enhance the quality of life for the inhabitants. Then, in 1882, West Bromwich 'arrived' in local government terms with the granting of borough status. There was a mayor, six aldermen and 18 councillors to oversee the management of all the trappings of municipal maturity – highways, gas, free library, sewerage, markets, baths and the park.

People such as Reuben Farley served their town in many ways out of a sense of fulfilling the 'civic gospel'. He rejected an opportunity for parliamentary ambition, preferring his local business enterprises and seeking to influence others to make contributions to improve local life.

It was the contributions of others seen in these photographs that did so much to make local people 'brighter and happy' by this sense of duty to the public.

DISTRICT HOSPITAL, Edward Street, construction took place between 1869–71. Demolished in 1981, a new hospital has been built on the site.

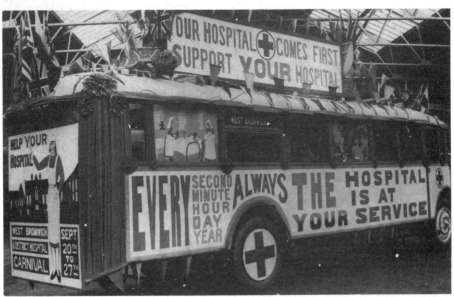

CORPORATION BUS decorated for the 1930 Hospital Carnival.

DISTRICT HOSPITAL STAFF shortly after the opening.

WEST BROMWICH INSTITUTE, Lodge Road, was the venue for a conference of municipal engineers and surveyors.

REUBEN FARLEY, five times mayor, devoted much time and effort to the improvement of local facilities. At the time of his death in 1899 he was described as 'the foremost figure in the public life of the town'.

FIRE STATION, Paradise Street – the mayor at the laying of the foundations in 1927.

SEWAGE WORKS, Friar Park, official opening in 1903.

COUNCILLOR JOE BAILEY in the grounds of the Labour Club in Sandwell Road.

NURSES' HOME, Lodge Road, in 1905 at the laying of the foundation stone which was observed by Masonic guests.

BOER WAR 1ST SOUTH STAFFORDSHIRE VOLUNTEERS of the Third Service (above) and First Service (below) West Bromwich 'E' Company.

THE FIRE SERVICE began as a volunteer brigade in 1881.

WIGMORE SCHOOL STAFF with Albert Hodder, superintendent, and his wife, matron, during the 1920s.

A HILL TOP TEACHER poses with her class in around 1915 while, below, the dancing lesson takes place.

SECTION SIX

The Once Rural Scene

For centuries West Bromwich was a scattered rural community. The Industrial Revolution changed all that, although half the land still remained in agricultural use until the mid-nineteenth century. With such close proximity to a large urban population the normal farming practices were replaced by products directly required by the town. There was a high demand for pork, dairy produce and potatoes. Before the appearance of motor vehicles, firms relied locally on horse power which needed hay and straw. By the 1880s there were only three dozen farmers left in the area.

David Christie Murray, in his Recollections published in 1908, noted that 'fifty years ago, or more, there was the most exquisite green fringe to that fire-rotted, smoke-stained, dirty mantle of the Black Country. In the extreme stillness of the summer fields, and more especially, as I seem to remember, in a certain memorable hush which came when afternoon was shading into evening, you could hear the clank of pig-iron which was being loaded into the boats on the canal at Bromford'.

Today the Sandwell Valley is the only survivor of Murray's 'plains of heaven within an easy ramble'. There, the award-winning restoration of a home farm and the nearby archaeological remains of Sandwell Priory give the visitor some idea of West Bromwich's origins.

WIGMORE FARM WAS later used as a riding school. The 'ironmonger's store', below, was demolished during the construction of the nearby motorway.

CHURCHFIELD HOUSE was built around 1758 by the Earl of Dartmouth for the incumbent of All Saints. It was twice altered and modernized but, by 1945, had become derelict. Below, the grounds of the house.

SANDWELL PARK FARM, home farm to the Earls of Dartmouth, seen here prior to the prize-winning restoration by the local council.

BEEHIVES at Sandwell Park Farm in the days before restoration.

COTTAGES AT BUSTLEHOLM MILL.

HAY TRUSSER, around 1920, operated by corn dealers Frederick and Robert Checkett.

OUTBUILDINGS AT LYNDON HOUSE pictured here in 1972 but since demolished.

COTTAGES IN PARK LANE on the West Bromwich/Handsworth boundary: (right) and rear views (below) of the now demolished buildings.

OAK HOUSE, 1891, prior to Reuben Farley's restoration.

LYTTLETON HALL, rebuilt in the eighteenth century, was run as a dairy farm until around 1950. Stables are seen on the left (below). It was demolished in 1974.

BIRD END COTTAGES and (below) a building converted from previously thatched cottages in Charlemont Road.

HOLLYOAK FARM, Stoney Lane, was a Tudor farmhouse demolished around 1945.

THATCHED COTTAGE, HAMSTEAD, around 1900.

BUSTLEHOLM MILL, prior to agricultural use, was a slitting-mill. Barn and stables (above) with the miller's house were demolished in around 1973.

GREAT BARR. Sun Dial House, now demolished, stood in Queslett Road, and Sycamore Farm (below) in the 1930s was on the Walsall, now Birmingham, Road.

On the Move

It was the need to improve road communications between Birmingham and Wolverhampton that led to the development of a town centre. The combination of the enclosure of the heath and the improvement of the turnpike road by Thomas Telford meant a High Street was quickly established. As early as 1835 an omnibus service was operating between West Bromwich and Birmingham. Next, a horse-drawn tramway was introduced, followed in turn by steam trams. When two of the latter stopped on local routes, Benjamin Crowther stepped in to fill the gap – many of his various vehicles are seen on the following pages. Eventually the council took over all the tramways within the Borough and electrified them. The trams were later replaced by Corporation buses.

Canals, which brought much of the original prosperity to the area, were superseded by the railways as a means of transporting freight. Passengers, on the other hand, were never seen as a priority on Black Country lines. The town's station closed down in 1972 and the track was removed to create a parkway and cycle route. This, however, will disappear with the coming of the Midland Metro rapid transport system.

Just as West Bromwich was historically on the great road to Chester and the main Holyhead mail route so, today, it still has good road links with motorway access.

IN THE 1890s Benjamin Crowther operated along the two routes previously plied by steam trams. The tram below, ready for the return journey to Smethwick, waits outside Arthur Brown's tobacconist shop.

CARRIAGE outside Oakwood House in Old Meeting Street.

TAME VALLEY CANAL seen from Crankhall Bridge in 1897. The high mounds of drift sand were later used for building purposes.

THE STEAM TRAM that operated along the Birmingham Road from 1883 to 1902, until replaced by the electric vehicles, seen below on their inaugural run.

CORPORATION MOTOR LORRY at the Hardware Depot around 1925.

WEST BROMWICH'S FIRST BUSES, 10 September 1914.

CORPORATION OMNIBUS No. 5 in 1920 and, below, one of three Leyland buses bought in 1937 for evaluation in tramway replacement.

DRIVER ERNEST CRUMP outside All Saints in around 1923. This bus was withdrawn from service in 1934 after 13 years' work.

HENRY BURNS at work, above, for Benjamin Crowther and, below, as a passenger in the front seat of the car driven by the Corporation's Transport Manager.

OAK LANE DEPOT displays its replacements for trams in March 1939.

FORMER PARADISE STREET nose to tail in the 1960s. Strangely this street is still listed on some bus timetables!

HENRY CHESSHIRE on his horse outside Oakwood House.

Shops and Streets

None of the anonymity of today's supermarket for the shops on the following pages. In many cases the owners and staff obligingly line up for the camera. By standing there in their working clothes they add something to the lettering and design of the shopfronts. One striking feature of many of these shops is the longevity of a particular business – there can be two or three generations of a family carrying on in a certain trade. Sometimes the shop remains a chemist's, butcher's or a draper's for a hundred years or more.

On some of the street scenes there stands that great institution of local life – the corner shop. Away from the bustle of the High Street there's something almost warm and informal even today in just popping out for a minute. Ned Williams in his fascinating 1986 study, Shop in the Black Country, *describes many of this 'style' of retail outlet.*

Many streets were the results of infilling but some came from the careful development of old estates. When The Lodge was sold, part of it was used for public buildings such as the town hall and hospital and the rest was given over to residential property. On early maps of the town many streets appeared as proposals never to be built!

Just as streets extended further from the town centre so local shops, often converted from houses, came into being – hence the long lists of just 'shopkeepers' in old trade directories.

HOLLOWAY BANK looking towards Wednesbury in around 1905. It was originally called Finchpath Hill but, by 1685, a 'hollow way' had been cut to ease the transportation of coal.

THERE WERE THREE BAKERS IN NEW STREET in around 1911 and, 20 years later, W.J. Harris was here at No. 10.

STUBBS, grocer and confectioner, on the corner of Mount Pleasant Street.

M5/M6 MOTORWAY JUNCTION under construction in 1968.

CROWTHERS, 1910 (above) and 1915 (below), ran trams, cabs, this garage, and a funeral business.

HILL TOP – ONE OF THE LAST REMAINING HOUSES built when the main road was called a 'holloway'. Below, old condemned cottages at Hall End in around 1927.

HARVILLS HAWTHORN in the 1930s.

RING O' BELLS near All Saints 1969 prior to its demolition for road widening.

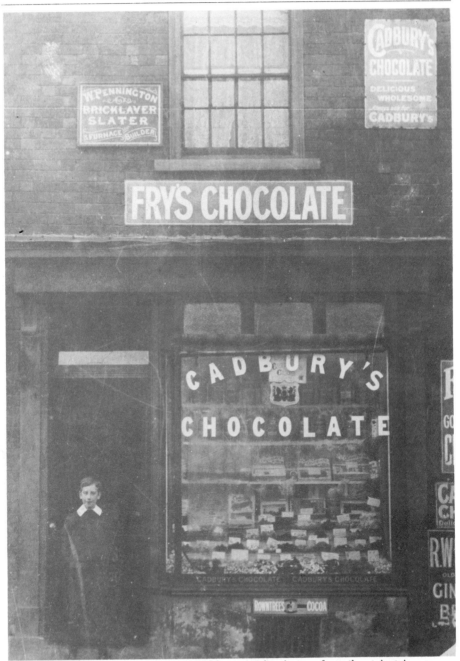

CONFECTIONER WILLIAM PENNINGTON, in 1920, seemed to have a few other talents!

TOLL-HOUSE on the corner of Slater Street in around 1900.

HILL TOP in around 1920.

WALSALL ROAD, now Birmingham Road, with construction (above) behind the shops of the Beacon Cinema.

WHEN JOHN LLOYD took over from Joseph Lloyd he ensured a continuous business for over 60 years at No. 4 New Street.

STAFF OUTSIDE THE PARADISE STREET TAILORS 1911. Later the firm moved onto the High Street.

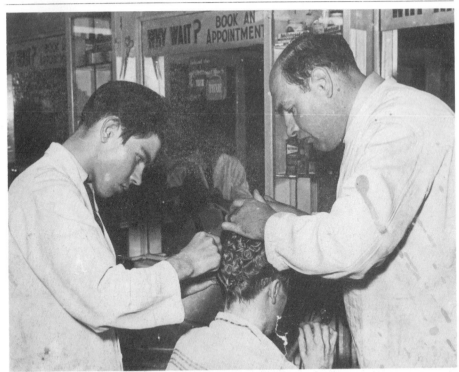

HAIRDRESSER THOMAS CAMMIES at work in his Paradise Street salon.

CART ready for deliveries from No. 220 Great Bridge Street.

NEW STREET. The backs of properties on one of the town's oldest streets which had been developed by 1816 along with Bratt and Lombard Streets.

THIS PHOTOGRAPHER later operated at other High Street premises before basing his business at Beeches Road.

PARADISE STREET looking into the entrance of Crowther's former yard in 1972 and, below, a wet day in the 1960s.

ST MICHAEL STREET, 1974, with the construction of the pedestrian subway under the future Ringway.

QUEEN STREET ROOF-TOPS around ten years before the 1969 clearance.

WALTER HENRY HARPER, second from left, and his wife, second from right, with their staff outside the St Michael Street premises.

GREAT BARR GROCER on the corner of Newton Road.

BRAYBROOK STREET once formed part of The Lyng.

DOVE STREET at its junction with Cross Street and Braybrook Street (below). All these nineteenth-century houses were cleared in the 1960s redevelopment.

DUDLEY STREET, around 1958, looking towards Great Bridge (above) and the other way along the former tramline to the Swan Inn (below).

WALSALL ROAD – bomb damage during 1940 air raid.

ANOTHER CROWTHER VEHICLE waiting to move off for Oldbury.

FREDERICK CARLESS first acquired No. 33 Bull Street before taking over the business of Thomas Woodward at Nos. 29–31 (as seen below in the 1900s). He was joined by his sons in the 1930s.

SECTION NINE

The Greens

Apart from the main heath there were other parts of West Bromwich that formed small open spaces. These survive today only as placenames for they too disappeared upon enclosure. They give a strange rural ring to the areas now covered in housing or industry.

Greets Green was once a piece of common land. Its name may originate from the 'Grete' that has given us nearby Great Bridge, or it may be some reference to a 'Great' Green having a number of halls such as Cop, Dunkirk and White.

Carter's Green on the other hand has a more interesting derivation. John Carter, a local constable, conducted a 1647 enquiry into the seizure of local goods during the English Civil War. It was said that this crossroads was the grisly setting for the burial of suicides each with a stake through the heart!

Other greens have their origins in the names of local families such as Rider and Mare. In the enclosure of 1804 the lord of the manor acquired an allotment of common land at Ryder's Green. Hall Green was another piece of wasteland that survived cultivation or enclosure for a long time but it was here that the Manor House was built. The present-day restored building is thought to date from around 1300. There are two other greens – Golds named from a fourteenth-century family of Golde, and Ireland from a local inhabitant of 1750.

CARTER'S GREEN. The clock tower was constructed as a tribute to Reuben Farley, within his lifetime, for all his work for the town.

A TRAM comes around past the Wesley Chapel built in 1875–76. More electric trams wait at the terminus (below).

THE ALLEN FAMILY ran the post office and drapery in Whitehall Road.

GREETS GREEN JUNIOR & INFANT SCHOOL. Built in 1876 and demolished in 1972.

THE PEARSON FAMILY of Whitehall Road, around 1900, previously lived in Cop Hall Street.

THE GREETS GREEN PUBLIC LIBRARY closed down in February 1975.

GREETS GREEN 1953 coronation parade.

MAYER'S GREEN – the Congregational Mission chapel pictured around two years before its demolition.

RYDERS GREEN. Canalside cottages at Eight Locks in July 1969 – now demolished.

HALL GREEN – scene of a dramatic restoration. Here we see the 1957 interior and exterior of the old Manor House.

SECTION TEN

Local Personalities

Some towns are inextricably linked with a famous individual who usually springs easily to mind. West Bromwich does not fall into that category. The one famous person who might qualify is only really acknowledged across the Atlantic. In America, statues salute Francis Asbury as one of the builders of the nation – the 'Prophet of the Long Road'.

'A prolific and vigorous novelist' was the acknowledgement paid to the Victorian writer, David Christie Murray, who was born in a house on the High Street. William Henley, the violinist, achieved a certain fame in his day but he could not break away and leave his native town. There was one person who did just that for the bright lights of Hollywood. The late Madeleine Carroll was a leading lady in films of the '30s and '40s. When the Tower Cinema opened at Carter's Green the timing was perfect – this local girl just happened to be the star of the first film shown, The Thirty-nine Steps. *Among her other triumphs was* The Prisoner of Zenda *in 1937.*

WILLIAM HENLEY, born at Hill Top in 1874, was dubbed the 'English Paganini' for, in his day, he was considered to be the only English violinist who possessed the 'fire and brilliancy' to match foreign artistes.

DAVID CHRISTIE MURRAY began his writing career as a reporter and war correspondent. He had many novels published and later wrote an autobiography (see below).

My dear Emmanuel
    Please accept this record of ups and downs,
failure, triumph, and adventure, with the friendliest
regard of
                    David Christie Murray

December 21st 1893

THE

MAKING OF A NOVELIST

OAKWOOD HOUSE, Old Meeting Street, was the home of Alderman Chesshire (opposite) for many years. When he retired to Hagely he had a house built in similar style and gave it the same name.

JOHN HENRY CHESSHIRE as mayor wearing his coronation uniform for the 1901 ceremony. He was chairman and managing director of Izons & Co.

WILLIAM IZON with his daughter, son-in-law and their two children outside The Lodge in 1860. William was the grandfather of John Henry Chesshire.

JAMES RICHARDS was town crier. Aside from his official duties he would, upon payment of a small sum, patrol the district and cry out the name of any lost child.

ACKNOWLEDGEMENTS

All the photographs are held by Sandwell Libraries. Firstly, the author would like to express thanks to all those people who have taken or donated photographs to the local studies collection especially in the last few years. Secondly thanks are due to John Maddison, in his dual roles as local studies officer for Sandwell and secretary of West Bromwich Civic Pride Association, for his encouragement and practical assistance during the compilation of this collection.